At the Fun Park

Written by Mary-Anne Creasy

Illustrated by Chantal Stewart

Flying Start
to Literacy®

Today we went to the fun park.

"This will be so much fun!" said my sister.

It was my first time at this park.

"Let's go on that ride," said my sister.
"It goes up and up and up."

The people on the ride were screaming.

"No," I said.
"I do not like that ride."

"And I do not like that ride," said Mum.

"Okay," said Dad.
"Let's go on the ride over there."

"This looks like a fun ride,"
said my sister.
"You go up a big hill,
then come down into the water."

People on this ride
were screaming too.

"No," I said.
"I do not like this ride."

"Let's go on this ride,"
I said.
"It goes around and around."

The people on this ride were not screaming.

"No," said my sister.
"This ride isn't fun."

"Here's a ride we can go on," said Dad.
"It just goes up and down."

I looked at the people on the ride — they looked happy.

Mum held my hand.
I looked up at her.
She didn't look happy.

"Are you okay, Mum?" I said.

"I do not like to go on rides," she said.

"I'll hold your hand on the ride," I said.

"Yes, okay," she said.

So we got on the ride
and held hands.
We all screamed and screamed,
and it was fun!